good answers
to tough questions

About Disasters

Written by Joy Berry

Copyright© Joy Berry, 2022
Originally Published, 1990

All rights are reserved.

No part of this book can be duplicated or used without the prior written permission of the copyright owner, except for the use of brief quotations from the book.

For inquiries or permission requests contact the publisher.

Published by Joy Berry Enterprises
www.joyberryenterprises.com

INTRODUCTION — 3

This book can answer questions about Disasters.

Natural Disasters, including:
- avalanches and landslides
- earthquakes
- floods
- hurricanes
- lightning
- tidal waves
- tornadoes
- volcanic eruptions

Man-Made Disasters, including:
- crowd hysteria
- explosions
- fires
- transportation accidents

4 — DISASTERS

A disaster is an extremely dangerous event that usually happens suddenly or without warning and affects many people.

Natural disasters are caused by nature.

Man-made disasters are caused by human beings.

DISASTERS

We can't always prevent disasters, but we can control how we respond to them. People who respond appropriately to disasters increase their chances of surviving them.

It is easier to respond appropriately if you are prepared for the possibility that a disaster could occur.

To prepare yourself for a disaster, first decide exactly where and how you would reunite with your parents and other family members if you became separated from them during a disaster.

Also, it might be a good idea to ask a relative or friend of the family who lives outside your area to serve as the contact person for your family in case of a disaster in your area. If the members of your family should become separated during a disaster in your area, each of you could phone the contact person. He or she could provide information that could help your family members find one another following a disaster.

To prepare yourself for a disaster, make sure your family has these emergency supplies on hand:
- flashlights with extra batteries
- candles with matches
- battery-operated radio with extra batteries
- first aid kit
- bottled water
- emergency food supplies
- sleeping bags or blankets

8 — DISASTERS

To prepare yourself for a disaster, find out about the area you live in or visit. Find out
- what kind of disasters occur in that particular area, and
- what emergency procedures should be followed for each disaster that could happen.

It is important for you to learn about the various kinds of disasters so that you will know what to expect and how to respond if you should experience one.

The remainder of this book will give you the basic information you need about natural and man-made disasters.

AVALANCHES AND LANDSLIDES

An avalanche or landslide is the swift movement of a large mass of material down a mountainside.

An avalanche or landslide can happen when a loud noise or movement jars a large mass of snow, ice, rocks, or earth that has collected on a steep slope. The jarring causes the mass to slide down the slope.

Avalanches and landslides occur in mountainous areas.

Snowslides can occur when large amounts of snow collect on the side of a mountain.

Rockslides can occur when heavy rain or melting snow makes the material on a mountainside loose and unstable.

Mudslides can occur when a long period of wet weather softens the earth on the side of a mountain.

An avalanche or landslide can quickly bury anything in its path.

Avoiding Avalanches and Landslides

- To avoid being in an avalanche or landslide, do these things:
- Check with local authorities when you visit mountainous areas. Find out where avalanches or landslides are likely to occur so you can avoid those areas.
- Comply with posted warnings about possible avalanches and landslides.
- Avoid hiking in mountainous areas where the ground seems loose or unstable.

Surviving Avalanches or Landslides

To survive an avalanche or landslide, do these things:
- Quickly observe the location and direction of the avalanche or landslide. Move quickly to either side of it, away from the center of the moving mass. Then tuck yourself into a tight ball to help protect your head and body from injury.
- Avoid trying to outrun an avalanche or landslide by moving ahead of it. A mass of snow or earth sliding down a mountainside moves faster than you can run.

EARTHQUAKES

An earthquake is a sudden movement of the crust of the earth.

An earthquake occurs when heat and pressure deep within the earth cause the earth's crust to crack and quickly change position.

Earthquakes can happen almost anywhere on the earth, including beneath the sea. Most occur near fault lines (seams in the earth's surface).

A large earthquake can damage or destroy bridges, roads, buildings, and other property.

Earthquakes also can damage water, power, and fuel lines, possibly causing flooding or fires.

Preparing for Earthquakes

To prepare for an earthquake, do these things:
- Determine which areas in each room of the house would be safest during an earthquake. Avoid places close to windows or large mirrors that could break during an earthquake. Also avoid places close to heavy furniture, cabinets, or appliances that could fall over.
- Pay close attention when you participate in emergency earthquake drills at your school. Also, ask your parents to have emergency earthquake drills at home.

Surviving Earthquakes

To survive an earthquake, do these things:
- If you are outdoors when the earthquake begins, stay there until the earthquake is over. Move as far away as possible from any power lines, buildings, or trees that could fall over.
- If you are indoors, stay there until the earthquake is over. Move as far away as possible from windows, large mirrors, heavy furniture, cabinets, and appliances that could fall over. If possible, get under a sturdy table or stand in a doorway. Stay away from stairways or elevators.

FLOODS

A flood is an excess of water in an area.

A flood can be caused by extremely heavy rainfall or the sudden melting of a snowpack. It can also be caused by a break in a dam or reservoir that has been damaged by an earthquake or heavy rains.

Floods often occur in lowland areas near streams or riverbeds. They can also occur in areas that are downstream from a reservoir or dam.

Floods can cause damage and destruction. A flash flood (a large volume of water flowing at high speeds) can damage or destroy anything in its path.

Preparing for and Surviving Floods

To prepare for a flood, determine the safest route to reach higher ground.

To survive a flood, take a safe route to higher ground or to another area. Stay away from the flooded area until it is safe to return. Do not walk or drive through floodwaters.

HURRICANES

A hurricane is a severe storm made up of swirling winds traveling at 75 miles per hour or more. Heavy rain usually accompanies a hurricane.

Hurricane-like storms occurring in certain parts of the world are called **tropical cyclones** or **typhoons**.

A hurricane can form when hot, moist air over the ocean rises and is replaced by cooler air. The cooler air rushes in from all directions and moves in a circular motion.

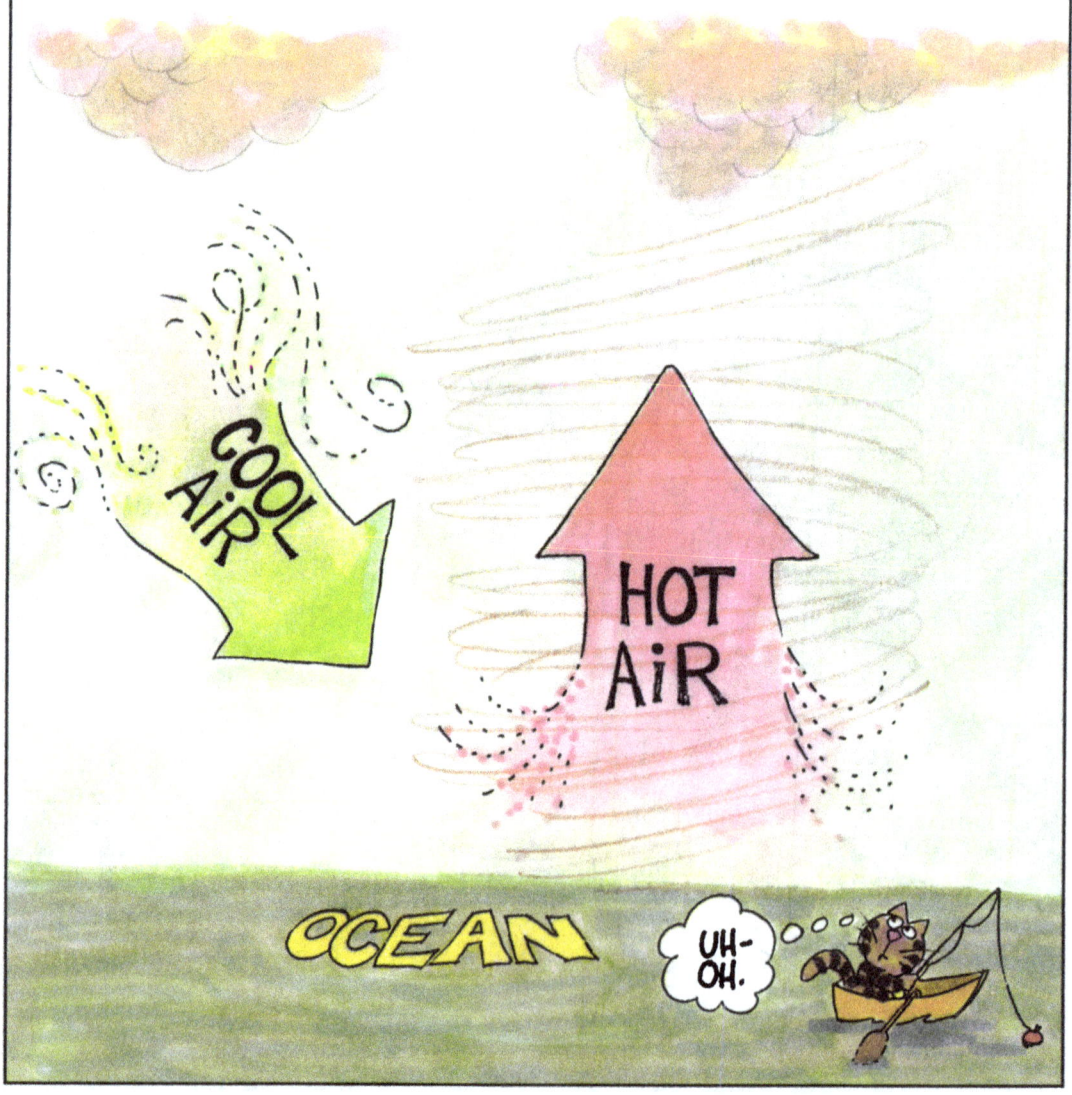

Hurricanes begin over the ocean, and some reach shore.

Hurricanes can blow the windows out of buildings and damage roofs. They can move heavy objects and uproot trees.

The rain that accompanies a hurricane can damage vegetation and cause flooding.

The large waves and high tides produced by hurricanes can wreck boats and other property along the shoreline.

Preparing for Hurricanes

To prepare for a hurricane, do these things:
- Determine which areas within your home are safe. Avoid places close to windows that could break.
- Pay attention to the TV or radio weather reports that provide hurricane warnings and information.
- Evacuate (leave) the area if local disaster authorities instruct you to do so.

Surviving a Hurricane

To survive a hurricane, do these things:
- If you are near sea level, move to higher ground.
- If you are in a mobile home, trailer, or temporary housing structure when you receive warning that a hurricane is approaching, quickly move to the nearest community disaster shelter. Find out from local police or fire officials where these shelters are located.
- Remain inside during a hurricane. Stay away from windows until the hurricane is over.

LIGHTNING

Lightning is a flash of electricity in the air.

Lightning is produced when wind and ice crystals within a cloud cause negative and positive electrical charges to separate.

What we see as lightning is simply a large spark that reunites these positive and negative charges.

Lightning comes from thunderclouds. Thunderclouds form when warm, moist air rises quickly into the cold air above it.

Lightning can start fires.

Lightning can severely shock animals and people.

Preparing for a Lightning Storm

To prepare for a lightning storm, remember these things:
- Lightning usually strikes the highest object in the area.
- Like electricity, lightning can be carried by metal and water.
- Like electricity, lightning can be stopped by glass, rubber, or wood.

Surviving a Lightning Storm

To survive a lightning storm, do these things:
- Go indoors as soon as a lightning storm begins. Stay away from plumbing fixtures, electric appliances, and telephones because these things are connected to outside pipes and wires that can cause lightning to travel indoors.
- If you are stranded outdoors during a lightning storm, stay away from tall trees and buildings that might be struck by lightning. Also, stay away from electrical wires and anything made of metal.
- The inside of a car or airplane is a safe shelter during a lightning storm as long as you do not touch any metal parts.
- If you are on a beach during a lightning storm, move away from the water. If you are in a flat or hilly area, lie face down in a dry ditch, gutter, or other low area.

TIDAL WAVES

A tidal wave is properly called a **tsunami**. It is an extremely large ocean wave that can be more than 20 feet high.

A tidal wave can be caused by an underwater earthquake or volcanic eruption.

Tidal waves occur on ocean shorelines located near underwater faults or volcanoes.

A tidal wave can destroy everything in its path as it floods the land and returns to the sea.

Preparing for and Surviving a Tidal Wave

To prepare for a tidal wave, pay attention to the TV and radio weather reports that provide tidal wave warnings and information.

To survive a tidal wave, use a safe route to get miles away from the shoreline. Do not return until local disaster authorities announce that it is safe to return.

TORNADOES

A tornado is a dark, funnel-shaped storm made up of whirling winds traveling as fast as 200 miles per hour or more.

Sometimes tornadoes are called **twisters** or (incorrectly) **cyclones**. Tornadoes occurring over water are called **waterspouts**.

Tornadoes are caused by violent thunderstorms that form when masses of warm, moist air meet cold air.

In the center (eye) of every tornado is a partial vacuum. When a tornado passes over a building, the air pressure inside the building becomes greater than the pressure outside. This can cause the walls of the building to blow outward and collapse.

A tornado can cause even very heavy objects to be blown about.

A tornado can destroy everything in its path.

Preparing for a Tornado

To prepare for a tornado, do these things:
- Determine exactly where you would go if you discover that a tornado is coming. The safest place is a storm shelter (a strong underground structure with a heavy door). The next safest place is a basement.
- If your home has no storm shelter or basement, seek shelter in a neighbor's shelter or basement or in a community shelter.
- Pay attention to the TV and radio weather reports that provide tornado warnings and information. Always move to a shelter whenever a tornado watch is announced on local radio or TV or by disaster authorities.

Surviving a Tornado

To survive a tornado, do these things:
- Go indoors during a tornado, if possible. Lie flat under a bed or mattress if you cannot be in a storm cellar or basement.
- Lie down in a ditch or other low spot if you are caught outdoors during a tornado. Even a gutter or curb can offer some protection. Avoid standing up so that you will not be hit by objects blowing about during the tornado.

VOLCANIC ERUPTIONS

A volcanic eruption is the ejection of hot gases and molten material from an opening in the earth's surface.

A volcano erupts when heat causes pressure to build up under the crust of the earth. The pressure seeks a release through the nearest opening. As the pressure escapes, it takes with it *magma* (rocks and other material that have been melted by extreme heat). Magma that reaches the surface of the earth is called *lava*.

Lava from a volcanic eruption can destroy everything in its path. It can also harm the water supply.

Ash from a volcanic eruption can make it difficult to breathe or see. It can also interfere with transportation and telephone, radio, and television communications.

Preparing for and Surviving a Volcanic Eruption

To prepare for a volcanic eruption, pay attention to TV and radio reports that provide volcano warnings and information. Follow instructions from local disaster authorities.

To survive a volcanic eruption, do these things:
- Use a safe route to travel miles away from the site of the eruption.
- Go indoors or seek shelter in a car if you are outdoors when volcanic ash begins to fall. If this is not possible, breathe through a damp cloth or dust mask, and protect your eyes by keeping them closed or by wearing goggles.

CROWD HYSTERIA

Crowd hysteria occurs when a large number of people experience excessive or uncontrolled emotions.

Sports events or concerts, or other gatherings in which the audience may become extremely emotional, can cause crowd hysteria.

Earthquakes, fires, explosions, or other life-threatening situations occurring where masses of people are gathered also can cause crowd hysteria.

Crowd hysteria usually results when many people rush to get to the same place at the same time. In most cases, the destination is a stage or an exit.

Crowd hysteria can cause people to be trampled, crushed, or suffocated.

Avoiding and Surviving Crowd Hysteria

To avoid crowd hysteria, avoid going to places where it might happen.

To survive crowd hysteria, do these things:
- Do not join a crowd of people who are all rushing toward the same place. Try to stay out of their way.
- Remain where you are if your location is not too dangerous and if it is not in the path of the crowd.

EXPLOSIONS

An explosion is a sudden, violent release of energy. Many explosions are accompanied by loud noise, flying debris, heat, light, and fire. Bombs, water heaters, and accumulated fumes from flammable substances such as natural gas or gasoline can cause explosions.

Surviving an Explosion

To survive an explosion, do these things:
- Close your eyes.
- Drop to the ground.
- Curl into a tight ball.
- Clasp your hands around the back of your neck.

FIRES

Fires started by people can become disasters. Such fires can happen when people become careless with anything that produces heat, sparks, or flames. They can also happen when a person maliciously sets something on fire. A person who does this is called an *arsonist*.

Preparing for a Fire

To prepare for a fire that could become a disaster, do these things:
- Find out what number you can call to reach the fire department. Post this number by the telephone. (In many areas, this number is 911.)
- Remind your parents to get a fire extinguisher for your house. Learn how to use the extinguisher properly and know where it is stored. Use a fire extinguisher only on *small* fires and only when there is a safe way out of the house or building.
- Plan escape routes from every room in your house so you will know how to exit safely if it catches on fire.

Surviving a Fire

To survive a fire, do these things:
- Leave a burning house as soon as possible. Feel every closed door before you open it. If the door feels hot, the fire is most likely on the other side of it. In this case, do not open the door.
- Stay close to the floor when you are leaving a burning structure so you can avoid breathing in any toxic smoke. If necessary, crawl on your hands and knees until you are out of the house.
- Do not run if your clothing catches on fire. Instead, cover your face with your hands, drop to the ground, and roll. Continue to roll until the fire is out.

TRANSPORTATION ACCIDENTS

Transportation accidents happen when a vehicle transporting people malfunctions or collides with another vehicle or object.

Transportation accidents that become disasters usually involve large vehicles such as planes, trains, ships, and buses.

Preparing for Transportation Accidents

To prepare for a transportation accident, do these things:
- Learn about the emergency exits and equipment on every vehicle you use. You can do this by reading the safety information provided, or you can talk to someone who can tell you what you need to know.
- Remain in your seat while the vehicle is moving.
- Always wear a safety belt if one is available.

MAN-MADE DISASTERS — 43

Surviving a Transportation Accident

To survive a transportation accident, do these things:
- Follow any emergency instructions given by the person in charge.
- Stay in your seat with your seat belt fastened. Place your face on your knees and wrap your hands around the back of your neck.
- Leave the vehicle through a safe exit in an orderly manner when it is safe to do so.

CONCLUSION

To survive any disaster, it is important to **stay calm**. People who panic often increase their chances of being injured.

To survive any disaster, it is important to **think before you act**. Focus your attention on keeping safe rather than on the disaster itself. People who are distracted by what is happening around them may forget to do the things that will help keep themselves and others safe.

46 — CONCLUSION

To survive any disaster, you need to follow the instructions of the people in charge. This is important for your own safety and for the safety of the people around you.

CONCLUSION — 47

To survive any disaster, obey any posted safety information signs. This is important for your own safety and the safety of the people around you.

CONCLUSION

You cannot always prevent a disaster. However, you can control how you respond to a disaster. In the end, that is what will help to keep you safe.

www.ingramcontent.com/pod-product-compliance
Lightning Source LLC
Chambersburg PA
CBHW081407070526
44583CB00020B/2717